MATTHEW RICE'S

COUNTRY YEAR

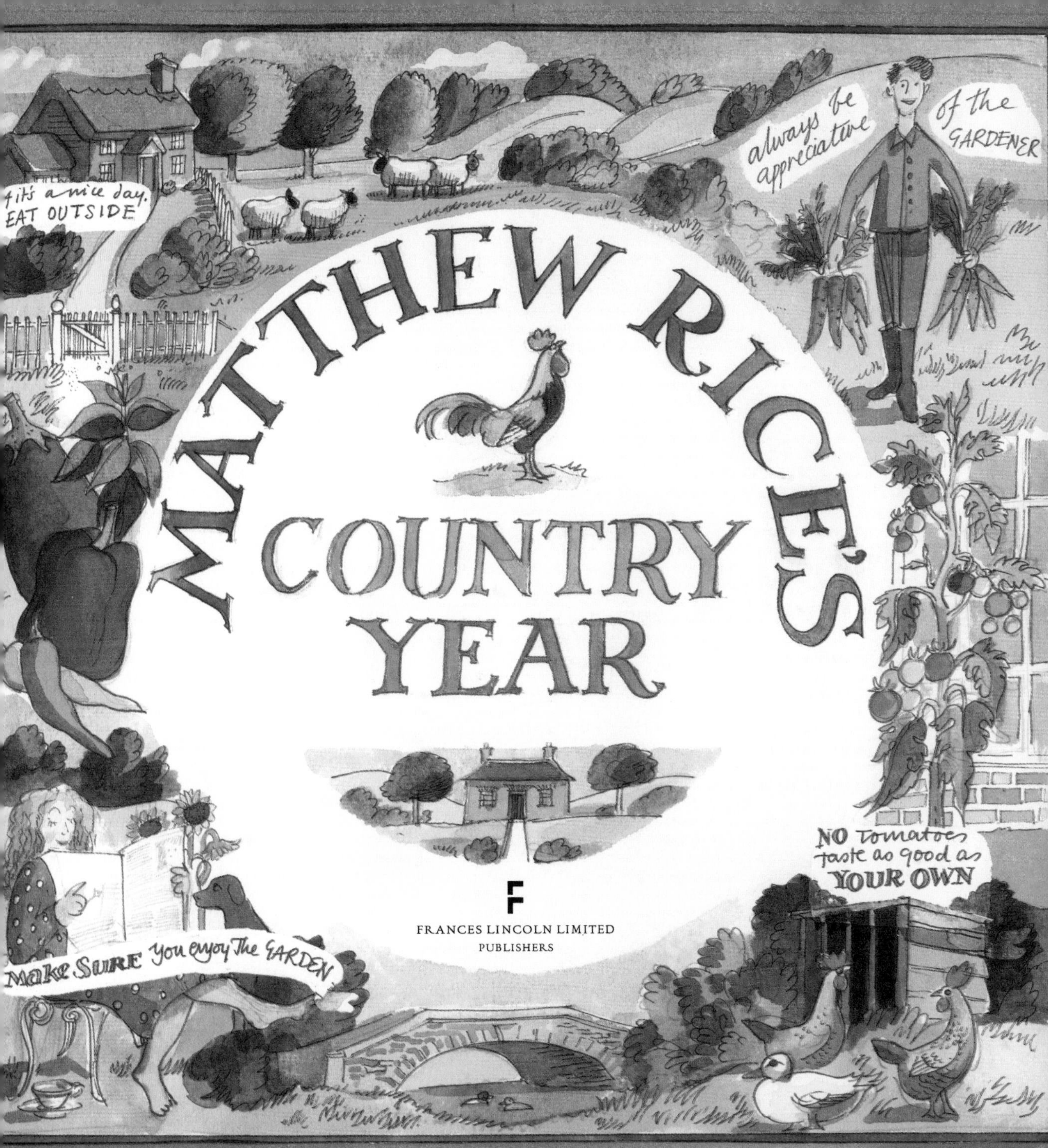

it's a nice day. EAT OUTSIDE

always be appreciative OF THE GARDENER

Make SURE you enjoy The GARDEN

NO Tomatoes taste as good as YOUR OWN

F

FRANCES LINCOLN LIMITED
PUBLISHERS

Frances Lincoln Limited
4 Torriano Mews
Torriano Avenue
London NW5 2RZ
www.franceslincoln.com

Matthew Rice's Country Year
Copyright © Frances Lincoln Limited 2010
Illustrations copyright © Matthew Rice 2010

A catalogue record for this book is available from
the British Library

ISBN: 978-0-7112-3168-9

Printed in China

First Frances Lincoln edition 2010

1 3 5 7 9 8 6 4 2

INTRODUCTION

The defining characteristic of living in the country is the change brought about by the seasons. Urbanites (or sub-urbanites) may spot the swallow, smell the lilac or shuffle through the leaves of autumn, but it is only for those immersed in the country that the experience of the year is so completely informed by developments that the months define.

The country dwellers' gumboots are almost year-round attachments, abandoned only when the frost is really hard or the ground parched by summer heat. Only the gardener will know when the soil *feels* warm enough to sow runner beans, or when it will break down enough to let you hoe the onions. And it is the day-to-day familiarity with what happens in the fields, woods and beaches – who flies through them, creeps about them or grows on them – that allows you, or I, to identify what really defines each month.

Whether utterly immersed in the country or exiled in town observing the seasons, the changing year makes sense of the sometimes rather specious tags of 'seasonality' in the greengrocery aisles of high street supermarkets.

Asparagus is the supermarkets' featured vegetable in May and June, but what is it like as a feathery fern in high summer? Or frost-bleached in December? Or underground when the first stubby shoots are heading for the surface? It is really only when you know all those stages too that the triumphant outburst of spears begging for their melted butter or Hollandaise makes total sense, crowning the asparagus' year.

The Jewish New Year starts in the autumn. Not to highlight the arrival of clever Hebrew students bustling to enrol at the beginning of the academic term, but because it is at the exact moment that one year's harvest is over and the next one's growth begins. While in Britain's harsh winters everything might appear to be dormant from October until April, the months are still marked with flowerings, arrivals and departures, and man-made seasonal events.

And it is outdoors that it is happening. Even on the gloomiest grey day there is something to see outside though the weather might seem to shout: 'Sit down and watch *Shakespeare in Love*, again...' True, you can see it through the glass well enough, but it will always feel better when you are actually out in it – even if it is just because of the anticipation of a crackling fire when you go back in.

So these pages have a few tempting calls to draw you out into the garden and the fields, or to make you think that a picnic is what you really *must* do today.

JANUARY

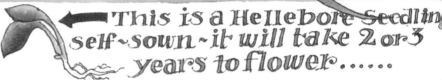

This is a Hellebore seedling self-sown ~ it will take 2 or 3 years to flower......

but it could be any colour.... this...

...or this...

....or this.

1   New Year's Day

2

After Christmas cut the leaves off your **Hellebores** to make STRONG new growth. they are the MOST Glamorous flowers for the NEW YEAR.

3

4

5

Epiphany

6

7

WINTER KITCHEN

MAKING BREAD
is less frightening
than it sounds
and **FRESH** bread
is just
what you want
with **SOUP**

Always make
STOCK of B
& SCR

8

9

10

11

SOUP is
Exactly what you
want for lunch on a
COLD WINTER
DAY ✦ In a heavy
Pan, Fry Onion, Garlic
and Ginger until
transparent, then
add the Potato and

Leek cut up small
and add some **STOCK**.
cook for FIFTEEN
minutes or until soft,
liquidize or Mash
and **ADD SOME**
Double cream ✿
DON'T FORGET
Salt and Pepper.

ROOT
GINGER

12

13

14

15

SNOWY AFTERNOON *(Indoors)*

16

17

18

MONOPOLY *takes up a* good long **TIME**  Teach those **bored** children to play **CHESS** (if you can)

19

20

PLAY CARDS WITH YOUR CHILDREN
It will sharpen their little minds & it is far better *than* television

21

22

BLUE hyacinths always smell best
but Pink and white look lovely so do them all
(Don't mix them though!)

Cake

Matthew Rice

23

USE ANYTHING that is big enough and watertight
enough to hold bulbs in. DON'T over water or let dry out
They SHOULD work every time (mine often end up as a straggly mess though)

24

25

a COPPER BREAD TIN [Ex P&O Liner] AND SIX LITTLE POTS of CYCLAMEN makes a really GLAMOROUS BIT of SPRING TO BRIGHTEN UP the KITCHEN

JANUARY IS THE BEST TIME TO PLANT A TREE. It may seem small now but even a 10 year old tree can be quite impressive, so START YOUNG

28

29

30

31

Plant NATIVE
species - look
to see what is
growing locally.
Oak trees can
Support over
200 species of
insect, bird,
moss etc

CHOPPER

LOOK AFTER THE TOOLS · CLEAN & OIL THEM and they will LAST FOR AGES

TROWEL

FORK

SECATEURS

ONION HOE

FEBRUARY

I

2

Wash out all your **POTS** and **SEED TRAYS** then your **SEEDLINGS** won't all go **MOULDY**. Break up the cracked pots and use them for **DRAINAGE** in the bottom of pots

Keep your tools in the shed not WET in the GARDEN

GARDEN SHED

4

5

6

7

fagiolo NANO

ORDER YOUR Seeds
When it seems that
spring will never come

8

9

10

I GERMINATE my seeds under a PLATE to keep them WET & DARK
It comes off as soon as they appear

This is a Tomato plant at 20 DAYS all on its OWN in a 3" POT

In The C19th SAILORS would decorate hearts with **SHELLS** for their sweethearts **ASHORE**

YOURS TILL The Waters Run DRY

11

12

13

14

Valentine's Day

Make (or Break) a **STRING of HEARTS**

VALENTINE'S DAY

15

16

VALENTINE COOKIES

Sift 10oz of Flour into a Large Bowl. Rub in 9oz of Softened Butter. Beat 2 Eggs in a separate bowl & add 6oz of soft Brown Sugar. Then add 2 tsp of Cinnamon, ½ tsp

of ginger, ½ tsp of nutmeg, ½ tsp ground cloves. Mix all the ingredients together. Roll out carefully until ¼ inch thick. Then using a heart-shaped cutter, cut out enough cookies for all your Loved ones. Bake on a buttered tray at 350°F for 8 mins.

SCRATCH in the letter of your LOVED ONE(S)

17

18

19

20

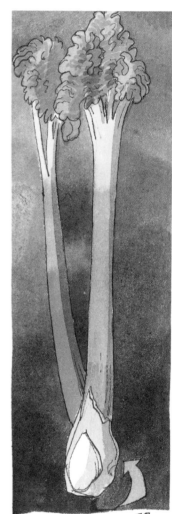

DON'T cut off
this bit it's the
SWEETEST
BIT of ALL

21

22

TO MAKE THE MOST DELICIOUS Rhubarb

very smart heart shaped baking dish from Bridgewater. ← cook this for VALENTINES DAY ♥♥♥

This is what to do: cut it into 2" sections and put into a baking dish with Lots of Vanilla sugar (keep a Vanilla Pod in a Jar of sugar all the time, very useful), thinly sliced ginger and the juice of an orange (you can grate the orange rind on it as well) cook in a medium heat in the oven for 20 minutes.
(Custard ESSENTIAL

unless you HATE it)

23

24

25

26

All Spring & Summer you will use ANY AMOUNT of HAZEL for stakes, supports & canes. Cut Hazel to ground level every 5-8 years (or higher if you have terrible rabbits) do this coppicing from DECEMBER TO MARCH YOU CANNOT HAVE ENOUGH.

A newly Cut Hazel is very Vulnerable to Rabbits GRAZING the young SHOOTS

27

28

29

Pen up a trio of bantams to breed from this spring...

that way undes
gentleman calles
will be kept at b
and the eggs you
will produce Pur
Bred Chicks
they'll be safe from FOXES

MARCH

I

2

3

4

COMB

EAR

WATTLES

CAPE

TAIL

HACKLES

BREAST

SECONDARIES

PRIMARIES

WING COVERTS

THIGH

SPURS

SPANGLED
(hamburghs,
Apenzellers)
etc

BARRED
(Marans,
Plymouth
Rock etc)

SPOTTED
(Millefleurs,
Sussex etc)

LACED
(Wyandottes,
Sebrights etc)

DOUBLE
LACED

CHICKEN
FEATHER
PATTERNS
[names of breeds that
have this plumage, in
various colours, in brackets]

5

6

7

8

SORREL is one
of the first useful things to
grow in the spring
WILD or DOMESTIC it makes the BEST soup.

... member of the family that Rhubarb
... come from. hence ... the
...KISH stems and long root. It will
... VERY easily

... may have to
... ke over it
... have
...ICKENS.

Fry some **GARLIC & ONION** in
olive oil (with Salt, pepper and a bit of sugar) **Add
a potato** (chopped into 1cm cubes) **When it
has softened add a big BUNCH
of sorrel, after 5 minutes pour
in Chicken stock**. Cook for 5 minutes.

You COULD, liquidize half of it and adding a
bit of cream in the bowls on the table
will make it even nicer

Matthew Rice

In the GREENHOUSE

DON'T leave the DOOR OPEN on a COLD DAY →

WINTER OUTSIDE

SPRING INSIDE

Rather a good place to work when it is nasty outside

We are not the only ones to like the warmth →

25

26

Although lovely, Hares do a lot of damage to young trees and crops (3 hares = 1 sheep in grazing terms)

Daffodils are picked when they're still in bud (they're called pencils) so they can travel. These are picked here in Norfolk, driven to Holland then by JET to New York

PENCIL

27

28

29

30

31

Daffodils: you
long for them to
arrive...

Then LONG for
them to go.

APRIL

1

April Fool's Day

2

3

LAMBS just love a bale of straw to play King of the Castle on. LAMB RACING (when they thrash around the field, LOVING being lambs) goes on for 20 minutes before dusk & is ENCHANTING

he wishes he hadn't escaped

4

5

6

7

Gros Vert de Laon

Violette

This is an incredibly sharp pointed one.
my mother brought the seeds in Sicily.

Grow Artichokes in the Kitchen garden or as a flower, if the purple petals appear, it's too late to eat it but it looks wonderful

Cut down the dead stalks by Christmas and protect with straw

lift the plants every 3 years and split off sets like this, they will make your new plants

a Duckling can swim the day it hatches BUT if it hatches under a hen it will get water-logged and sink, the mother duck oils their feathers & they FLOAT

Rabbits breed
all year but
these are
EASTER
BUNNIES

Beware there are baby foxes about as WELL

10

11

12

13

14

Melt 10oz of GOOD chocolate in either a Bain-Marie or a saucepan with a bowl inside it. Meanwhile polish the surface of your Easter egg mould with cotton wool (this will ensure a shiny finish). **Paint** layers of chocolate into your mould. Leave to cool, then fill the egg shells with your favourite chocolates, seal with melted chocolate. Decorate with ribbons and fresh flowers.

They are VERY GOOD LAYERS

White Leghorn lay white eggs

a Rhode Island Red — lays a TINTED egg

MARANS lay a very brown egg

15

16

17

18

KEEP YOUR Chickens safe from FOXES and other undesirables.

Here is a good BROODY hen

She will be happy to hatch and look after chicks, ducklings or goslings

Chicks take 21 days to hatch

Ducks take 30 days

CHICKENS & EGGS

different breeds of chicken lay different coloured eggs

These are MARANS, they lay the BROWNEST of brown eggs

LEGHORN

ARUACANA

ORPINGTON

19

20

21

22

HERB OMELETTE

Beat 3 eggs, salt, pepper & a small handful of fresh herbs (Mint, Marjoram chives, parsley) Melt a walnut sized piece of butter in a frying pan, pour in the eggs, when it starts to set, fold in half and turn over - cook for another minute and eat it.

The **FIRST** green tips of spring herbs and yellowest eggs [free range hens lay their best eggs now because of the spring grass] make the best omelette of The Year

Blackbird
nests in a
hedge or a
low tree.
4~6
eggs

Pheasant 8~15
eggs laid in a nest
on the ground on the
edge of a
wood or in
a hedge

Oystercatcher
4~5 eggs on the beach
marsh or moor

Mallard 6~12 eggs
by the edge
of the pond.

25

26

27

28

Everybody loves to hear the first cuckoo of spring but most people don't recognize them by sight • Here he is
He flies like a small hawk

Don't give up hope • SPRING IS HERE (any day now.....)

29

30

MAY

GHOST MOTH

BARN OWL ON PATROL

LONG EARED OWL

DRINKER MOTH

MAY IS SO OFTEN the most Beautiful MONT... as the temperature rises so nature gets goi... and a night-time walk can be M... Rewarding

LISTE...

for the liquid noisy trillin... of the lookin... tut

WONDE... FUL sound... NIGHTIN...

1

2

3

4

Here are 5 main *types* of *flower* found in *Cultivated tulips* My favourite tulip is Queen of the night plant This black tulip to grow up through PURPLE SAGE (looks *wonderful*)

watch out for flower loving children!

TULIP TIME

Lily Flowered

Double

Single

5

6

7

8

9

10

11

Parrot

Fringed

BUTTERFLIES & BUGS

MONARCH

A Nice Sunny Day

Brings Them OUT

This is a WATERBOATMAN
he scoots about on
PONDS

SPANISH FESTOON

BRIMSTONE

LARGE BLUE

This rather FIERCE looking character is in fact harmless it's a SHIELD BUG

LADYBIRD LARVAE also BITE

Five Spot Ladybird

Red Admiral

SMALL TORTOISESHELL

some painted Ladies migrate from MOROCCO

The UNLOVED stinging nettle is a useful foodstuff for

12

13

14

15

DRAGONFLIES

are lovely

BUT their nymphs (young)

BITE

16

17

18

19

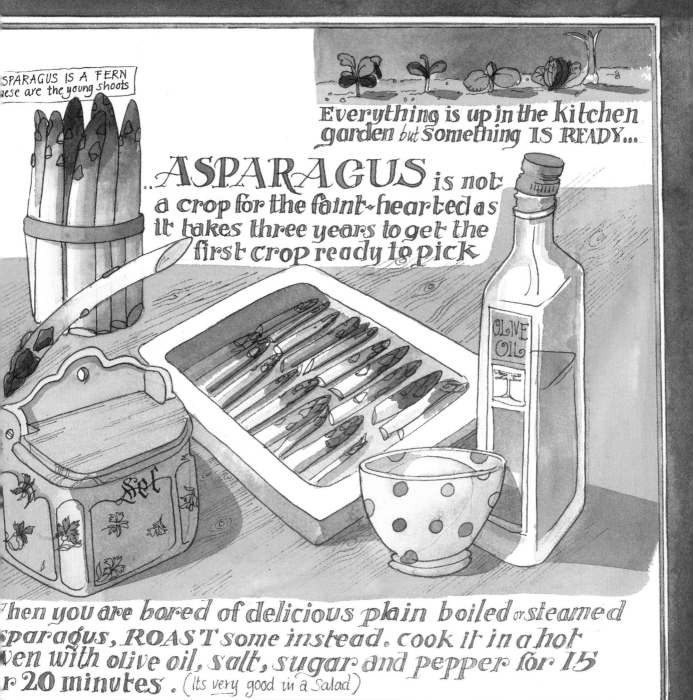

ASPARAGUS IS A FERN these are the young shoots

Everything is up in the kitchen garden *but* Something IS READY...

..ASPARAGUS is not a crop for the faint-hearted as it takes three years to get the first crop ready to pick

OLIVE OIL

Sel

When you are bored of delicious plain boiled *or* steamed asparagus, ROAST some instead. cook it in a hot oven with olive oil, salt, sugar and pepper for 15 or 20 minutes. (Its _very_ good in a Salad)

20

21

a wooden HIVE

a straw Bee Skep

Honey on the Comb

NOBODY LOOKS REALLY good in BeeKeeping KIT

OVER 30,000 BEES can live in one HIVE

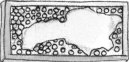

22

23

24

25

26

27

28

Oak Apple Day

29

30

31

FROGS & TOADS

FROGS are green ~ooth & SLIMY

FROGSPAWN comes in Lumps

TOAD SPAWN is in STRINGS

TOADS are BROWN · DRY & WARTY they also squirt nasty toad-juice on you if you pick them up

JUNE

HOORAY! SWEET PEAS are READY
(if you remembered to plant them last OCT/NOV...)

CHATSWORTH
(modern but still
scented)

1

2

3

The Best Smelling
MATUCANA

PAINTED
LADY first
bred in
1737

4

5

6

Make an outside kitchen – very little equipment required!

A SLAB on some BRICKS or an UPTURNED DUSTBIN & a GRILL and you can boil, fry or Grill anything

cook on embers raked over from The fire

7

8

9

10

KEBABS are a
very good project
for Junior cooks.
THREAD onion,
pepper, aubergine, courgette & chicken
with bayleaves between and GRILL on that
fire (if they come from your garden, they'll
taste
TWICE
as
good

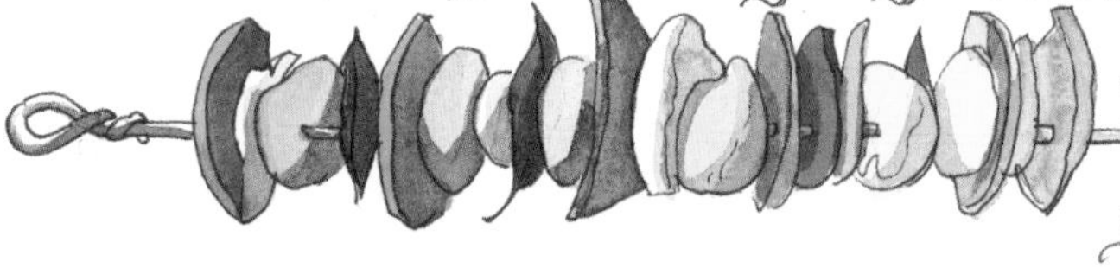

11

12

13

14

Basil keeps the Whitefly away

Sow some **BASIL** seed every WEEK

a Roast Chicken can't get enough **ROSEMARY**

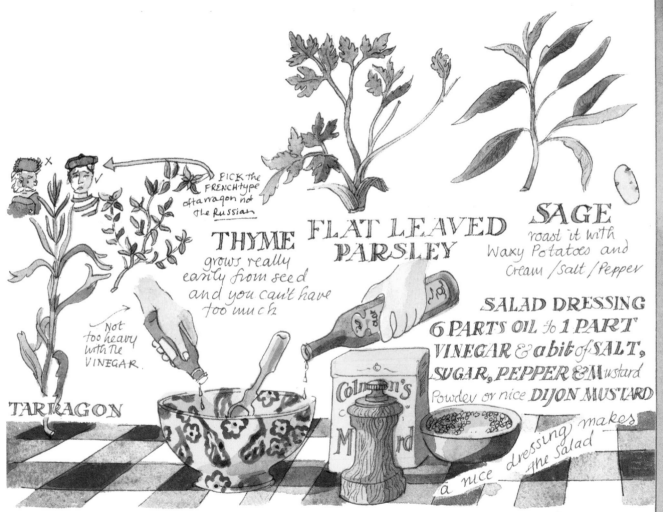

PICK the FRENCH type of tarragon not The Russian

THYME
grows really early from seed and you can't have too much

FLAT LEAVED PARSLEY

SAGE
roast it with Waxy Potatoes and Cream / Salt / Pepper

Not too heavy with The VINEGAR.

TARRAGON

Colman's Mustard

SALAD DRESSING
6 PARTS OIL to **1 PART**
VINEGAR & a bit of **SALT**,
SUGAR, PEPPER & Mustard
Powder or nice **DIJON MUSTARD**

a nice dressing makes The Salad

SALADS & HERBS

16

17

18

19

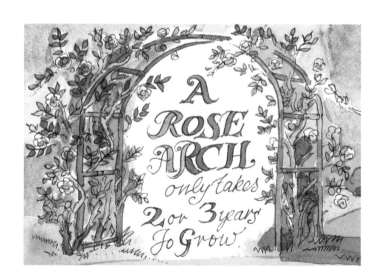

A
ROSE
ARCH
only takes
2 or 3 years
to Grow.

20

21

Comte de Chambord

22

Rosa
Moyesii

(This one's from china)

23

Albertine
new dawn

24

25

26

27

28

29

30

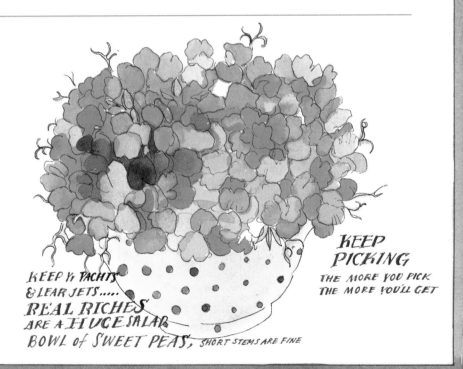

KEEP y YACHTS
& LEAR JETS.....
REAL RICHES
ARE A HUGE SALAD
BOWL of SWEET PEAS, SHORT STEMS ARE FINE

KEEP
PICKING
THE MORE YOU PICK
THE MORE YOU'LL GET

1

2

3

4

Chickens
can
clear up
CRUMBS

5

6

7

8

ABOUT ONCE a year Peaches are so cheap you can buy a box for £5. MAKE PEACH CHUTNEY.

Peaches (Peeled + Chopped)
Sultanas & Raisins
Demerara Sug
Salt
pts malt vinegar
whole Blanched Almonds
nger (½ oz)
onions chopped fine (well small, anyway)

* Combine all ingredients in a preserving pan and simmer for 1½ hours until thick stirring from time to time

When ready put in JARS

FEMALE

baby Courgette

MALE

COURGETTE FLOWERS

are one of the most delicious things to eat in the high summer. You can take as many male flowers as you like without affecting the supply of courgettes (but females are particularly good)

Make a batter with flour (very little) beer, egg and a little salt. Split any female flowers then dip them all in batter and fry quickly in ½" (1.5cm) of Olive Oil Drain on Newspaper put onto a Courgette leaf and sprinkle with SALT

10

11

12

13

14

15

St Swithin's Day

Cut in half last

1

2
dig out
Choke
with a
sharp
teaspoon

3

Fry ARTICHOKES
hearts the same
way. Heres how
to clean them
1 TRIM 2 SCOOP
3. THAT'S IT

16

17

18

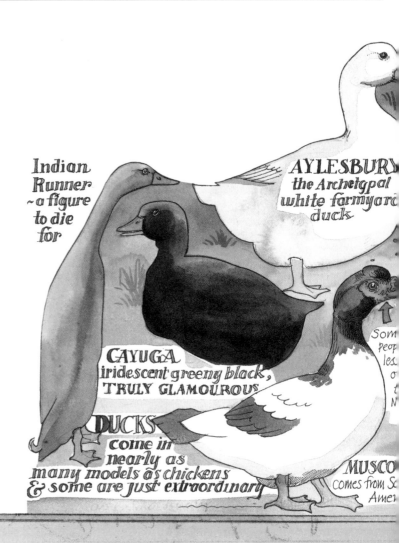

Indian
Runner
~ a figure
to die
for

AYLESBURY
the Archetypal
white farmyard
duck

CAYUGA
iridescent greeny black,
TRULY GLAMOUROUS

DUCKS
come in
nearly as
many models as chickens
& some are just extraordinary

Som
peop
les
o
t
N

MUSCO
comes from S
Amer

DUCKS are a treat in the garden but NO friend to a row of young CABBAGES as I have found to my cost

19

20

21

1week

ducklings are very quick to grow

5weeks

22

23

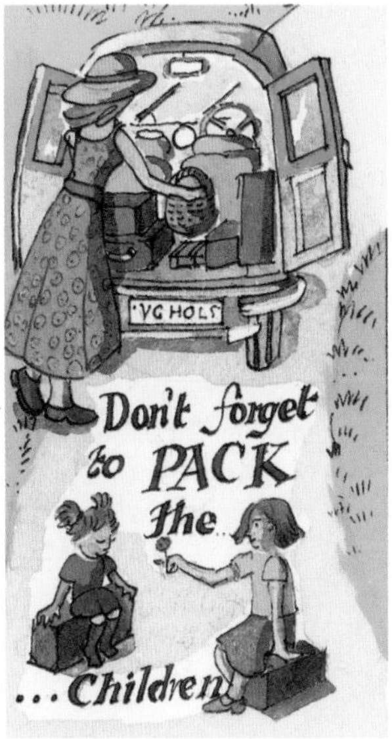
YG HOLS
Don't forget to PACK the ...Children

24

25

MACKEREL only worth eating Fresh

26

27

Cook them on fire on the beach [DON'T MAKE THE KITCHEN SMELLY] Cool the wine in the SEA don't forget the LEMONS (or, even more importantly, the CORKSCREW)

Just before you leave home ... SOW some LATE VEG in the garden (french beans, Beetroot & salad) They'll be ready in SEPTEMBER · when everything else is gone

28

29

30

31

1

2

3

4

KEEP HIM away

A Basket of Garden Produce makes the most SPECIAL PRESENT

VEGETABLE PATCH

eating food IN SEASON does WONDERS for your Cooking

EGG   PLANT
is v.
Hard
to
GROW

a Variety of Tomato called
Marmande
is meaty &
Delicious

USE YOUR ONIONS
While They are GREEN

There's no Point in
growing a Dull type
of tomato. you can
buy them in the
SUPERMARKET

7

8

It's Worth growing
Peppers if you live
somewhere
HOT

Always sprinkle a
bit of SUGAR on
your Tomatoes~it
brings out Their
TASTE

9

10

11

12

13

14

Faro

Cory

Dahlias *light up the garden when all the borders are looking* TATTY & GRIM
Keep Picking .... *the more you pick ; the more they Flower*

Bishop of Llandaff

CHAT NOIR

Jescott Julie

This is a REALLY good Idea....

AN OUTDOOR SINK IN The Middle OF THE KITCHEN GARDEN MEANS REALLY clean VEGETABLES & MARI TALLY SIGNIFICANTLY, IT KEEPS the MUD OUT OF THE KITCHEN

16

17

18

19

20

21

22

23

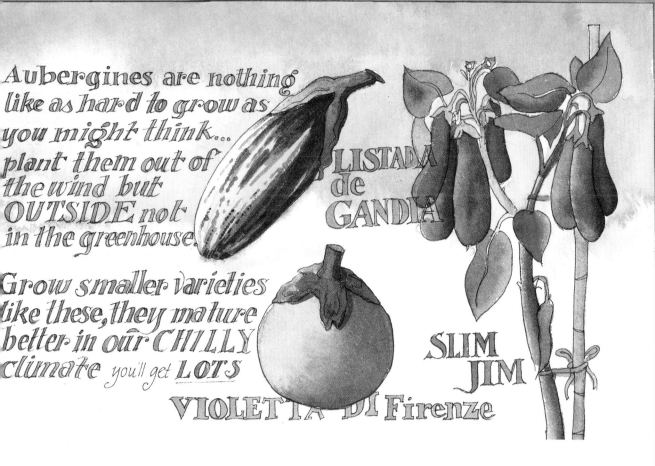

Aubergines are nothing like as hard to grow as you might think... plant them out of the wind but OUTSIDE not in the greenhouse.

Grow smaller varieties like these, they mature better in our CHILLY climate *you'll get* LOTS

LISTADA de GANDIA

SLIM JIM

VIOLETTA DI Firenze

24

25

26

27

28

29

30

31

Evening Sun on blissful AUGUST DAY

RUSHING in to cook the sweet corn right now Because.....

Every minute After the cob is picked the sugars in the corn are turning into starch. SO the quicker it goes into boiling water the more DELICIOUSLY SWEET it will be

September is the month when there is EVERYTHING to eat in the garden, it MAY look a little FRAYED AROUND the EDGES but this is the time for a FEAST

SEPTEMBER

1

2

3

4

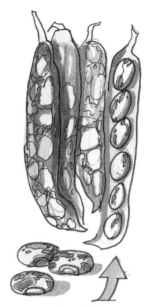

Borlotti beans, seen in every Italian **market but not much in England.** Shell them when semi-dry and cook with garlic olive oil and stock for 45 minutes then sprinkle with lemon rind.

5

6

DANGER
←

KEEP the cockles
in a bucket of
SALTED water
to SPIT out
their SAND & GRIT

WATCH OUT for
ANY that are at
ALL OPEN it
means the little
fish inside are
DEAD &
could give you
a terrible
TUMMY ACHE

7

8

COCKLING is best where SAND & MUD meet. TAKE A RAKE to SAVE YOUR FINGERNAILS..

hese OYSTERCATCHERS re also AFTER COCKLES.. ey have JUST come back to the COAST from their NLAND BREEDING GROUNDS

9

10

11

12

13

HARVEST TIME, as well as wonderful weather [I hope] means you can see all the birds that have been hidden by the standing corn (not just birds)

early blackberries

14

15

The ORCHARD

No Apples taste Better than the ones from your OWN TREE

If you Prune TOO hard, you will get all GROWTH & NO fruit

BUSH.

CORDON

ESPALIER

Fruit trees can be trained in all sorts of odd wa

17

18

19

APPLES need to be
stored in the cool & dry
and must not
TOUCH EACH OTHER

MAKE APPLE JUICE or CIDER
with excess fruit
(Watch out for home-
made cider)

20

21

22

23

PTEMBER = RAVISHING WEATHER, hedges full of Rosehips
thorn & brambles, Frothy with summer growth. Farmers cut them NOW
ch is easy but destructive. Better to do it every other year (in Winter)

angled inwards. This

'A' Shaped profile makes best use of the area

Blackberries, autumn food to help birds survive the winter

The BANK is now BARE no cover for ground nesting birds next spring

HARD
HTY
the hedge

Plenty of Cover for Winter Shelter

BAD

GOOD

25

26

27

28

29

30

The most GLAMOROUS
fruit of the
SUMMER

Fierce pruning
will get you
more fruit

OCTOBER

KITES

I went to HONG KONG when I was 18 (1980) and was thrilled with my first sighting of whirling, thermal riding KITES ↖.

Now there's no need to go EAST, they are 20 miles West of LONDON due to Successful INTRODUCTIONS in 1989 to the Chilterns. IN FACT one has now been seen in HACKNEY so they will be back to their OLD HAUNTS

I

2

3

4

5

6

7

8

SOMETIMES PEOPLE GET TO LOOK LIKE THEIR ANIMALS

NEVER *forget how important* FARM ANIMALS ARE to us

...but then DUCKS are rather an ODD family

BLUE SWEDISH

INDIAN RUNNER

ROUEN

MUSCOVY DUCK

CALL DUCK

FARM ANIMALS

11

12

13

14

15

16

17

SPARTAN
crisp with V Red
shiny skin

Why plant a tree that doesn't fruit when you can plant one that DOES?

ASHMEADS KERNEL
delicious

BASE   STALK
CAVITY

NAMING
OF
PARTS

BASIN

APEX   EYE

DISCOVERY
very early but rather
loved by wasps
BEWARE

18

19

20

21

RED LEGGED
PARTRIDGE

GREY
PARTRIDGE

PHEASANT

22

23

make sure you TWIST &
PULL OUT the sinews
else the
Legs are not
worth
eating

Nobody wants a pink
rubbery bird. Stuff
them with cottage
cheese, lemon &
rosemary, salt + Pepper
cook on their SIDES with
butter paper over them and White wine in
the pan around them for 40 mins then 20 mins
paper **off** turned onto their backs.

Similar product,
different packaging

24

25

26

27

PUMPKIN & SQUASH

Custard SQUASH

sweet Dumpling SQUASH

CROOKNECK SQUASH

Horrid-looking Bumpy one.

Cut a butternut or acorn squash in half-scoop up the seeds-put in Butter, sugar, salt & pepper o BAKE for ½ hour

The Pumpkin who HATED Halloween

Atlantic Giant is the BIGGEST of the pumpkins & they have grown to 100lb (which makes a v big PIE)

PUMPKIN SOUP

Cut up about 2lb of Pumpkin into 1" cubes with no peel or pulp- fry 2 cloves of Garlic and 2 onions chopped small in ½ butter/½ olive oil—when soft add pumpkin, pepper. salt and a dessertspoon of sugar! cook for 5 mins - add chicken stock then cook for 20 minutes

Grey Rind-Orange flesh is CROWN PRINCE = best for looking with

28

29

30

31
Hallowe'en

NOVEMBER

1   All Saints' Day

2   All Souls' Day

BE CAREFUL

of FIREWORKS bu
not SO CAREFUL that
your children aren
allowed SPARKLERS
because they are w
makes NOV 5th wh
it is ....

3

4

5

6

CHERRY

MAPLE

OAK

HICKORY

WILLOW

7

8

9

10

Any
Digging
you can do
now will
make
Starting again
in the Spring
easier.

II

I2

RISOTTO These are **CEPS** or **PORCINI** otherwise known as **Penny Buns**

Chop up some onion & garlic and fry in 50% olive oil/50% butter until golden. Add uncooked ARBORIO rice and fry till translucent. Add white wine and stock by the cupful (one after the other) until cooked. Fry chopped up Porcini for 5 minutes with Salt & Pepper & 1 Chilli, add to Risotto after it has cooked for 10 minutes. (Grate Parmesan on top)

FUNGI are still available this month **DON'T PICK THEM** unless you are really **SURE** (Get a Book)

These lurid purple ones are **FIELD BLEWITS**

13

14

15

16

LOGS

can easily become an obsession · will they last all winter? have we got the right type-size? YOU CAN'T HAVE TOO MANY

PINE
Burns Quickly but Spits a bit

BEECH
Burns very well - splits nicely too

OAK
needs to be dry to burn well but rather slowly

ASH is Best of all. burns wet or dry

ALDER
very good and splits well

APPLE or **PEAR** are lovely & smell very good as they burn

That's enough logs

19

20

DON'T Prune The ROSES TOO hard or they will...

not survive the harsh winter weather ~ Prune them LOW in the spring) if you live Somewhere very Cold

THESE CANADA GEESE are off South to get a bit of SUN

21

22

23

24

EAT VEG in SEASON they're what's best—ANYWAY do you REALLY want to eat french beans or new potatoes when it's COLD?

GARLIC £5·00

FENLAND CELERY

SPANISH LEMONS

November is a good month for WINTER VEG

AVERY

SWEDE 40p

FRUIT

GRILL SOME CHICORY with Salt, Pepper & Olive oil— eat with some Lemon Juice over it

25

26

27

28

29

a fieldfare

This month sees the arrival of flocks of fieldfares from Scandinavia. They are HUNGRY & LOVE berries SO If you want some HOLLY for Christmas, cut it NOW & hang it up in the shed.

30

Big Flocks of Fieldfares & Redwings
fly over from Scandanavia
for our Mild Winter
and Berries

Fingers
crossed
for Snow

MISTLETOE

grows particularly well on
old APPLE or PEAR TREE
and Poplars. hang it above
a strategic door for
FESTIVE KISSING

DECEMBER

I

2

3

4

MAGNOLIA LEAVES
MANAGE to look GLAMOROUSLY
TROPICAL & CHRISTMASSY
AS WELL

5

6

7

8

9

SNOWMEN can
SOMETIMES ALARM
Sensitive DOGS

others are
UNMOVED

11

12

13

AVOID BREAKING a LEG
or similar
BEFORE CHRISTMAS

Seasonal FAMILY activities

LONGON ➤ **TURKEYS** used to be walked from **NORFOLK** to Smithfield Market for Christmas (they had shoes made of Tar & Sand to save their feet on the journey)

14

15

16

17

18

19

20

21

22

23

24   Christmas Eve

25

26

MULLED WINE

FOR a cold winter evening and for rather SUB-STAND wine whose taste can be DISGUISED

RECIPE

In a Pan WARM 1 bottle of wine · 2 small oranges, 10 lumps of Sugar · 1 glass of brandy · 4 Cloves 1 stick Cinnamon and 4 berries of Allspice

27

28

29

30

31

NOTES